Life's

MW00452809

Overcoming Addictions

- ➤ Author's Note

- ➤ Preface

- ➤ The Value of Time (poem)

- ➤ 1 – Growing up

- ➤ 2 – The Way We Think

- ➤ 3 – Changing Lifestyles

- ➤ 4 – Living in the Now

- ➤ 5 – Power of Choice

- ➤ 6 – Purpose and Meaning

- ➤ 7 – Life After Addiction

- ➤ Acknowledgments

Author's Note

About the Author;

I was raised in a single family home by a loving and hard working mother. I was the eldest of four children, two sisters and one brother. We grew up on the poor side of town in Joliet, Illinois, a working man's town about thirty-five miles south of Chicago.

Going to school I never looked ahead, no career thoughts, no thoughts of college. I always looked up to the guys that were standing around on the corners. The tough guys. I wanted to be like them because nobody ever messed with them. They had the respect of the streets. Going to jail was like a badge of honor to me.

My mother worked two jobs, gone most of the time, leaving a lot of free time for uncontrollable kids.

I was always mischievous and always on the wrong side of the law. I married young and after twenty-seven years it ended in divorce. I worked in construction all of my life. I always drank alcohol, and then cocaine came into my life. Fun at first, mostly recreational, but it soon became a habit. And then the monster known as crack came upon the scene, and all hell broke loose.

After many stints in both Will County and Cook County jails, I did a three-year term in state prison, but that did not deter my addiction. Finally, the federal government stepped in and sent me to prison for a long enough time to get my head straight. I reluctantly self-surrendered to Milan Federal Correction facility in Milan, Michigan.

On the way to the prison I was smoking crack, drinking, and smoking cigarettes all the way there right up to the front door.

When I arrived, nine hours late, I took a drink of brandy, a slug of beer, lit up my last hit of crack, and my last drag of a cigarette told my ride, "Well I'll see you when I see you." I walked into that federal prison, went right to the hole, and right then and there I knew I was done with drugs.

Preface

If I have learned anything in over fifty years of a drug infected, criminal life style, it's that knowledge will not change your behavior. Only desire will do that. One must somehow develop a stronger desire to do the right things than to continue a self-destructive life style. I knew that if I took care of myself first, then everything else would work out. I learned to always rationally self-analyze all situations, seeing the consequences of my actions before I acted.

I have lost everything I owned over and over again. Spent many years in prison. Wasted many years in crack houses. Been through all the ups and downs in a whirlwind life of addiction. Honesty must be the foundation of your change. Being truthful with yourself is imperative in becoming the best person you can be. I developed a value of time.

I learned to appreciate everyday of life, and to live in the now, and stop wasting time worrying about the past or the future. Just live, and be the best you can at the present time.

The Value of Time

I am in this situation now
Because I did not value time
Stuck in a dream, chasing a ghost
I knew I would never find

Before I got to know myself
It was easier to lie
To hide the hurt and emptiness
To smile instead of cry

Think about being in a place
Having no hours in the day
Everyday you wake up
It is the beginning of yesterday

I have lived most my life in darkness
Never looking ahead
Sometimes I would see the light
But choose the darkness instead

Imagine after all the struggles and all the pain
I came to find
That while I pursued this fight with darkness
It was the light I left behind

Chapter One

Growing up

When I was nine years old my family moved to the east side of Joliet, the poor side of town. It was a large old scary house next to some railroad tracks. All of the kids grew up a little scared, especially at night. There was a wooded area down near the tracks that we all referred to as the bum's camp.

We used to go out at night and sneak into a local brewery by crawling up an old coal conveyor to steal booze. Then we would go down to the bum's camp and drink until we got sick. We would hang out down there and do all kinds of mischievous things.

My friends and I started sniffing glue at this time. The bum's camp was our place to get high.

We used to call it "cracking the bag." We would sniff glue, drink booze, and howl at the moon.

We would take guns we had and shoot them off. It's a miracle we did not shoot one another. It was a fun at that time of my life. This started when I was twelve and continued until I was fourteen.

There were never any thoughts of the future. No career expectations, or thoughts of raising a family. I never dreamed of what I would do for a living. My sister who is two years younger than me did most of the cooking. My mom had to work late most of the time. We ate a lot of spaghetti-O's and cereal for supper. We were embarrassed to bring most people over to our house. Not because it was dirty, but because we did not have much. We walked on plywood floors until one of my uncles got a deal on some used carpet that an old movie theater was throwing out. When you came into our house you wanted popcorn.

I am the oldest of four children raised by my mother, although my mother and father were not divorced when I was a child. I can never remember my father spending a night in the same house. Most of my friends were also raised in single parent homes.

When I was twelve years old my mom must have noticed a change in me, and so she asked my uncle to take me camping for the summer with his family. I have a cousin, Bobby, same age as me, and we were the best of friends growing up. We did everything together at family gatherings, holidays, and birthdays. I was excited to go. I had never been camping, fishing, or anything like that.

One day my cousin and I were at the beach swimming and this older kid was picking on him. So I pushed him down and kicked him. To my surprise my cousin loudly started yelling at me. "What did you do that for? Well go ahead kick him, kick him down like a hood."

I was devastated. I thought I was doing something that any good friend would do. I was hurt and shocked. Still today I can hear his words as if he were standing right next to me. It was at that exact moment that I knew I was different. I was not good enough, inferior, less than, out of place. After that we did not speak to each other.

A couple of days later my aunt and uncle asked me to come into the tent and explained to me that they brought me along to be a companion to Bob, and if things were not working out it was better for me to leave. That afternoon my uncle drove me home. It was an hour drive, and he never said a word to me.

I was so happy to be back in the hood where I felt like I belonged. I developed an attitude of anger and resentment towards anybody that lived on the west side, the rich side of town, or anybody born with the proverbial golden spoon. This feeling stayed with me for the next forty years.

My new heroes became the guys hanging out on the street corners, the tough guys. They were respected and looked up to in the hood. When they got into trouble and went to jail most of us viewed it as a badge of honor. They showed a young kid like me some interest. I was proud to be friends with them.

I can recall learning how to steal at an early age. During my summer breaks from high school, 1965, 66, 67, I worked at the horse race tracks in Chicago where my father was the head of security. He taught me the hustle there and how to steal money.

I would steal on average $100 a day. Soon I got connected with the *three-card-monte* players, and I made an extra $100 per week with them. The last summer I worked there I would arrive early to deal poker. I earned $8.00 per hour plus tips. One thing those horse owners did not know was that the cards were marked. My dad would get them for $125.00 a deck cellophane wrapped. Also he had a shill sitting in the game that knew the marks and they would split the profits. It was an exciting time in my life. I had more money than anybody I knew. It felt good. I never believed I was doing anything wrong.

Stealing became normal behavior to me. While in my senior year of high school I stole three hundred suits from the semi-trailer trucks parked next to our house. I stuffed them in an old junk car that was abandoned close to my house. Then I went to school and first thing in the morning I asked my homeroom teacher if he could get me three days off of school. He questioned me. I explained to him that I suddenly got a hold of some suits, and I needed to get rid of them quickly, and if he would help me I would give him a suit.

He agreed and told the dean that he caught me smoking for the second time in the school bathroom, so the dean expelled me for three days. I then took orders and sold all 300 suits, mostly to the teachers at school. The day I graduated I left the auditorium, took off the gown, went to the local liquor store, bought a quart of beer, and went to the bum's camp to toast my accomplishment.

I bought my first car in the summer of 1968. A '57 Chevy, it was primed and ready to paint when I wrecked it. Three of my neighborhood friends and I were out drinking and smoking weed. It was raining and I was coming down a huge hill towards a stop light. I thought I could make the green, but I was mistaken. I hit a car that car hit another car, and that car hit another car. No one was hurt. My friends took off and left me there to face to police. I got some tickets and they towed the car home. I did not have insurance, actually I did not even know about insurance at that time.

I ended up losing my license. So my father, who I was still working with at the race track, took me to the DMV to get another license under another name so I could drive up to the race track, and he could sleep. I wrecked a different car under the false name coming out of a tavern. Now I was going to court getting sued by four different insurance companies under two different names. Lucky for me, I got my draft notice in the mail. I showed that to the judge, and he threw everything out.

My sisters and their friends pushing that old wrecked 57 Chevy around the alley while one of them steered. I could hear them having fun pretending to be driving.

Although we did not have much, we were a fun family. My sisters and brother always seemed to be playing practical jokes on one another. I'll never forget one time when lightning struck our TV antenna and fried our television.

My mom bought a new TV that came with a wireless remote. At that time wireless remotes were just coming out. I had never seen one. It was the late sixties. I had just come home and the whole family was sitting in the living room watching the new TV.

My youngest sister said to me, "Hey we got a new TV and guess what? All you have to do is say the channel and it will go there."

I said, "No way."

She said, "Try it."

So I did, I looked at the TV and said out loud, "Seven," and lo and behold it turned to channel seven. I was amazed. Unbeknownst to me she was standing behind me with the remote.

She said, "Try it again."

I was totally enthralled. I quickly said, "Two," and the TV turned to channel two. I could hear and see everybody laughing extremely hard. I started laughing also, not knowing what was going on. Then they told me, and all of us had a good laugh.

When I think of times like that I always smile.

Chapter Two

The Way We Think

After graduating from high school, I started construction ironworking which was like joining another bunch of guys who had no problem breaking the law. I quickly fit in and became very good at my trade. I was elected to the executive board and also appointed to the apprenticeship committee. I put a lot of pressure on myself to live up to the expectations of being someone with clout. I felt lost most of the time not knowing how to act with the popularity.

I got married and had three children. I strived to be the family father. I bought a pop-up camper and joined an outdoors club. I took the family camping on the three-day weekends. Even though I never knew anything about camping.

I coached little league baseball and got to be real good at coaching baseball. I went to most of the events in their early lives.

I was drinking after work with the guys practically daily. Trying to be one of the guys. In the trade of ironworking at that time, if you weren't in with the tavern crowd you were an outcast.

Then I started sniffing powder cocaine, but usually just on weekends. It felt fantastic at first. If I was tipsy after drinking, it would sober me up. I used to joke that they should give everyone a line of coke when they leave the bar to get home safely. As my addiction grew, powder cocaine was not enough. I started smoking crack cocaine. It was then that my life went right down the sewer.

When I got heavily steeped in addiction my only thoughts were of getting high.

I did not think about my own well-being, family, or even world events. It's as if you are a blind caterpillar living in a cocoon filled with lies and deceit.

I remember a time when I was selling some stolen meat to a restaurant owner and during the transaction he mentioned the fact that Al Gore had lost the presidential election although he got 300,000 more votes.

I acted like I knew what he was talking about, but in reality I didn't even know the election was going on or who was running for office. To top that ... I did not even care.

My addicted way of thinking had become a compulsive obsession with getting high. I was so totally focused on getting high that nothing else mattered. That kind of thought process becomes an addiction in itself.

Once I was shopping at a K-Mart when I bumped my shin on a large cart that had a 36 inch Curtis Mathis television on it. As I rubbed my shin with one hand, I rested my other hand on the TV. A young salesman came up to me and asked, "May I help you with that, sir?"

I immediately responded, "Why yes you can young man." He then proceeded to wheel the cart out to my car and helped me load it in my trunk. I tipped him my last five dollars and promptly phoned the dope man.

When I finally decided to get clean, I had to concentrate on changing the way I thought and the way I viewed myself in life.

For example, when I am walking down a street and see a ladder leaning up against a house, I do not think that someone is painting their house, like a normal person would. I first wonder how much money I could get for that ladder. It is not easy to overcome that way of thinking. It will take time and effort.

You must learn how to turn knowledge into wisdom. Experience alone will not bring you wisdom.

You must be aware of your thoughts and where they are taking you at all times.

Recognize your errors in thinking and strive to change them.

Understanding is not realization; understanding is the one thing that keeps you confident in the choices you make. Knowledge alone cannot change your behavior nor will it bring you happiness. Not even experience will change your behavior.

The only thing that will change your behavior is your desire to be a different person. Albert Einstein once said, "The definition of insanity is doing the same thing and expecting different results."

My father's absence in my early life left me with a lack of social skills and no ability to deal with authority figures. I lack a certain self-confidence and have to fight feelings of being alone in the world. I looked to the wrong people for security.

Negative thoughts of yourself will lead to undesirable outcomes in your life, as well as your relationships with your spouse, children, and family.

Keeping a humble attitude and a "gratitude list" handy will help you to strive to do the right thing. You may want to have things on your gratitude list like: family, having food, having a place to stay, having clothes, and basically things in your life that you have been blessed with. You must also learn to change the way you see events in your life. I can remember many times making mountains out of mole-hills by not comprehending just how important or unimportant certain things actually are.

For example, I was once speeding, running stop signs, going through red lights just to be the first one at the bar after work. I would notice the guys I passed up in such a hurry were only a few seconds behind me.

I could have seriously injured someone or myself.

Life is so very precious, not to be taken lightly. Your life is filled with unforeseen opportunities, and wonderful times of happiness yet to share. Don't take the risk of never having the chance to experience them.

Most of the time we create our own problems in life by the way we see events in our life unfold. Your thoughts, self-image, and your self-awareness are all connected to the way you think of yourself.

Negative thinking will make you miserable and people will avoid you, making you even angrier and more miserable, and then the law of attraction comes into play. Remember... misery loves company.

Make sure that the achievements that you strive for in life are meaningful.

If they aren't meaningful, then they become a useless waste of time and will make no difference in your life at all.

All too often we get overwhelmed by our jobs. You are not what you do! Never let what you do for a living define you as a person. Do not think any more or less of yourself because of your job. Most parents always ask their children "What are you going to do for a living?" when they should be asking "What kind of person do you want to be?" Work to live; do not live to work.

Many frustrations come from the fact that most of us don't even know what we want out of life. Then when we attain the material things that we thought would make us happy we find that we are not satisfied with those things. We want more and, when we get more we are still not happy because we worry about losing the things we now have. We fail to see that this kind of false sense of achievement in life is exactly the thing that which imprisons us.

We tend to live in our own illusion of the world. In that illusion we get addicted to a multitude of things. Not all addictions are associated with drugs.

There are a few types of addiction that are equally negative such as: creating chaos, ego boosting, needing attention, living in misery. Know that all addictions begin in the mind. Usually they are diversions from an underlying problem corresponding with a sense of fear... fear of knowledge of self, afraid to look in the mirror, afraid to realize just who we are and what we stand for in this world.

We must always keep in mind that life is not meant to be lived in suffering over a parade of regrets, anxieties, or all the things you wish you could do over.

Your mind wants to be free of obligations, and free from any other thoughts that lower your self-esteem.

Uncontrollable desires, emotional outbursts, and knee-jerk

reactions soon will become things of the past.

As you practice self-control in your thinking, keep

your thoughts on your well-being. Getting to know yourself

better everyday will take practice, but your time will never

be better spent.

Time is not always easy on the mind. Hanging onto

the negative in life will make you miserable.

Positive thoughts are an open door to life's

happiness. There are no ordinary moments in life. They are

all unique and special. The secret to enjoying these times in

your life is not found in having more, but in developing the

capacity to enjoy less. You must have a simple awareness of

what is really significant. The ultimate perfection of your life

is unfolding at all times.

Choose to be happy.

Chapter Three

Changing Lifestyles

Because of the lifestyle I chose to lead I would get hassled by the police constantly. I always complained about them. But in reality, they were doing the right thing. After a while living in the drug world, the police will know all about you. You will be on a first name basis with most of the cops that work the drug unit.

I once got pulled over for stopping too long at a stop sign. They made me get out of my car and searched the vehicle; it did not matter that I had not given them permission. After they did not find anything, I got a ticket for stopping too long at the stop sign. I went to court and the judge threw the case out. The same officer pulled me over a few weeks after my court date and had asked, "Why did you go to court for that bullshit ticket, you got me in trouble?"

I asked him, "Why do you guys constantly pull me over?"

He said, "You know why, because you are always up to no good."

And he was right.

When I retold the story about the ticket to my family they were shocked at the police officer's behavior. But I corrected them, by saying he was telling me that if I want to continue to do drugs, do it in another town. Now that I am sober I applaud these actions because I was always on bullshit. I was always getting pulled over whether I was driving or riding in a car. All the police knew all the drug addicts by sight.

The hardest thing about changing lifestyles is breaking away from the reckless relationships you make along the way. These people will make you think that because you share a similar lifestyle, the relationship is acceptable.

Your recognition, and consequently your self-worth, seems to come from the success of your capers or as the addict sub-culture calls them *"licks."*

In the late 70's I heard about that novelty invisible ink. I then went to the bank and opened an account for $50. I took a handful of deposit slips home and filled them out in my name and account number each for $1000.00. When the ink disappeared I returned to the bank and put them back in the compartment they came from, generally they were stored in a kiosk in the center floor of the lobby. In about 4 days I called the bank and got my account balance. To my surprise it was $5050.00. As I suspected, the machine read both numbers when the deposit went through it. I immediately went to the bank and closed the account. I purposely did not fill out a withdrawal slip. I then went to another local bank and did the same thing. I was not even in the bank when the money was going into my account.

I could hardly wait to brag about my success to all the other players in this twisted addict world. It seemed perfect, but like all licks, once others hear about the success of your lick they all attempt do the same thing and almost immediately the banks change policies. Much like the cash card lick. When ATM's were in their infancy. I would offer people money for their cash card.

And ask them to not report it lost for a couple of days. I would then go to the bank the card was drawn from and put the card in the ATM. When it prompted you to make a transaction I would push deposit then put in the amount, at that point deposit an empty envelope.

The ATM machine then asks if you'd like to make another transaction. I would press withdrawal, as long it was less than half the amount you falsely deposited you would get the cash. These types of activities gave me a sense of importance in the world I lived in. I felt like a big man amongst my drug associates. To make matters worse I did not even feel remorse, but rather a twisted sense of pride.

One of the most troublesome imbalances in life is the disparity between your actual daily life and the dream you have for your life. We all have a dream about what our lives should be and the way we want to be acknowledged by others.

We have an unlimited supply of imagination, and it is always equipped to fulfill our dreams and create our destinies.

Except when you are in the grip of addiction you get separated from your dreams, imagination, and thoughts for your future. Your only focus is on your addiction. I never knew where I was going to sleep, or when I was going to eat. I was a blind caterpillar living in an eternal cocoon of lies and deceit. Life was all about getting high.

If you continue in this negative lifestyle you will close many doors that you may someday wish were open. A police record, and bad credit, are just two of the things that will follow you as long as you live. Job applications, trying to secure a mortgage loan on a house, getting credit cards, and buying a new car all become difficult. After my divorce I had $30,000.00 cash from my share of property and could not get a bank to give me a savings account.

When you are not doing the things you need to reach your goals it becomes a source of frustration that can evolve into depression or some kind of adverse addiction.

But most of the time it is just a feeling in your heart that you know something is off.

You realize you want your life to be different, but can't seem to take that first step.

It is as if there is something that is keeping you from reaching that next plateau in life.

Addiction is considered by many to be a symptom of what could be an accumulation of underlying problems, such as fear of success, lack of self-confidence, low self-esteem, or just a general feeling of being less than adequate.

You have to be attentive to your inner feelings. Constantly evaluate just who you want to be, and then take the necessary steps to get there. Realize that in taking the steps to reach any goal there will be some wrong turns along the way. Those turns will give you cherished knowledge and experience to better recognize and accept your limitations, as well as strengths in navigating through difficult situations. Getting to know yourself in times of trouble is the first step to obtaining the courage to release that familiar lifestyle.

Do not get discouraged. Remember if the path you are on has no obstacles then it probably doesn't lead anywhere.

Be vigilant not to become short-sighted when recognizing your weaknesses. I can't begin to count the times that I said to myself, "Well, I will only have one drink then go home". That never seemed to work out. I always stayed for more and when I felt a little buzzed I would then want to get high. Nothing could stand in the way of that obsession. I would often justify getting high by telling myself, "I work hard, I deserve it," or "It's my money." So I would go to the crack house and end up spending all my money.

I would stay out all night, miss work the next day, cause problems at home, and end up borrowing money for gas and food to be able to go to work. I would go through the week with a distraught heavy heart until next pay day. Then say "I am only going to have one".

Always weigh the cost versus the pleasure of your actions. Stay focused on the good and positive things around you every day. Be grateful for the things you have and thankful for the gifts that life has bestowed upon you. Never be too overconfident or arrogant and start to think you are better than anybody else just because you seem to be on the right track.

Remember if you are not moving forward, even if on the right track, you will get run over. Know that you are in a daily fight for your life, so be persistent when it comes to your wellbeing.

Every life has its own song to sing, and although some songs may seem louder, not one is more important than the other. Be respectful of other's feelings. Keep the spirit of forgiveness in your heart. Most of all give yourself

the gift of forgiveness. It will relieve you of the stress and

anger you have towards anybody you perceive has wronged

you. Realize nobody

is perfect.

They say in Alcoholics Anonymous that having

resentments is like drinking poison and expecting the other

person to die. You must let go of these feelings, it is the only

way you can grow and not cloud your mind with useless

thoughts that only matter to you. Most of the time the

person that you are harboring these hidden resentments

against is not even aware of the situation.

When you live your life just going through the

motions to please someone else, doing what they expect of

you, you become detached from your own dreams. When

you let someone else's life become your life, you are

actually cheating yourself out of living the life you were

meant to live. When it comes to choices in your life make certain that you are making the choice you want, independent of external pressures.

You might spend too much time trying to make others proud of you and not enough time focusing on what is important to you. This often makes you feel a dissatisfaction in yourself, and these negative feelings will greatly affect the way you look at yourself.

I can recall doing things just because I thought I would get noticed as a great guy, only to have no one seem to care. It's very disheartening.

You must give some powerful thought to the person *you* are as well as the person *you* want to become.

What's more important is to take the necessary steps to bridge that gap.

When you are able to discipline your desires you will feel an empowerment that gives you strength to conquer various types of temptation that may arise. As you practice your self-control you will gain the kind of self-esteem that will make you the person you will be proud of; you will learn to love yourself. Once you achieve this attitude you will rarely be defeated by self-defeating thoughts.

Albert Einstein once said, "No problem can be solved by the same mindset that created it." I believe he is saying that if you want to change your life you must begin with the way you think. Honesty must be the foundation of this change.

Start an honest relationship with yourself by continuous self-talk. Keep presence of mind that you are most important person in your life.

Let calmness flow into your life. Never be anxious for anything.

Let life unfold as it is destined to be. Know that life is too short to feel beaten. Time is too valuable to waste it on anything that is not improving your life. Embrace the change in your thinking. Understand that failure does not present itself in making mistakes, rather in not rectifying them. Habitually do the right thing even when no one is looking. Your reward will be greater than you ever thought possible.

You will feel a sensation that will put a smile on your face that nothing can take it away. You also will feel a renewed confidence in yourself.

Always remember that having a good name is the most precious thing you can possess.

Chapter Four

Living in the Now

Something happened that made me realize the significance of living in the now. It started in September 2007 when I was incarcerated in Milan Federal Prison. I was in great physical condition. I worked in the prison industry making good money, and things were going pretty good, plus I was getting close to my out date, which was the end of 2012. Life was good considering.

One day I awoke to swollen ankles. I went to the prison doctor, and they started testing trying to find out what was going on. After three years of visits and tests they had diagnosed me with kidney cancer.

I will never forget that day. I was at work, my (C.O.) corrections officer had informed me that I was to report to the medical office after work. I thought that was peculiar because at that time the medical staff was usually gone.

As the only inmate in the infirmary the doctor called me right in his office. He explained I had a solid mass carcinoma attached to my left kidney. I was stunned, shocked, in disbelief. My thoughts were racing so fast I could not grab them to form any kind of response. He told me the psychologist was standing by if I needed to talk to her. I asked "Just how bad is it"?

He explained, "Well you are a 60 year old man with a history of drug and alcohol abuse, so let's just say it's not good".

I then asked, "What's next"?

He stated that he would put me in for approval for an outside surgical procedure. I knew I did not have a good chance for approval.

The Bureau of Prisons will consider the cost of this procedure against my out date. I was a 60 year old inmate with kidney cancer and my release date was in a little less than 3 years. They would continue to push it back until I was released and then it would be too late for me.

I pleaded with the doctor to please get me on the list for an outside doctor visit. I mentioned my name to the doctor and he said "I know who you are Mr. Carey". I replied, "No you actually don't. To you I'm inmate number 22247-424. I have a family and a life I would like to get back to. I need to make some amends before I die."

On my way back to my cell, my thoughts scattered in a labyrinth of unanswerable questions, I realized the pulverizing fact that I had cancer.

I felt helpless, to make matters worse I had no one to call. I kept thinking this cancer was growing inside me and I could not make the wheels of medical care in the prison system turn quicker. I could never recall feeling so alone in the world. My children were hurt and angry with me. I had been gone so long that my sisters went on with their lives and we had lost that close contact. My brother had passed away in a tragic construction accident. I laid in my bunk and I cried out to God.

Realizing I did not know how to pray correctly, which I mentioned in my prayers, I just kept saying the name Jesus, over and over and over again. It was five months later that I went for the surgery. The surgeon informed me that if the tumor was too bad he would have to remove my kidney.

The operation went great. The doctor only had to remove about 1/3 of my kidney.

When the doctor came to see me he said he thought the tumor had reduced in size. Thank God! At the time I was released in Sept 2012 I remained cancer free.

Although we live in the body, our struggle is with the mind, a constant war with our own thoughts and desires that shape our daily emotions and actions. After all, we are what we think. We can take the best of situations and make them terrible and vice versa. We can twist our minds to think some of the most off-the-wall things, and then when we stop and reflect upon our actions and thoughts we often feel foolish. Most of our future is controlled by our thoughts and the choices we make today.

John Milton wrote in his epic book **_Paradise Lost_,** *"The mind is a place of itself and in itself it can make a heaven of a hell or a hell of a heaven"*.

I know many times I used to stew about a situation and let it fester in my mind until I was ready to explode. I would get so upset that I would get physically ill.

My whole countenance would change. Like a Dr. Jekyll and Mr. Hyde. Usually after a while I would simmer down and realize the situation was not nearly as bad as I had imagined.

You must comprehend that you cannot worry about situations you can't control. Especially other people's thoughts and behavior's. Let peace resonate in your thoughts by trying never to assume someone else's thoughts. Always try to think the best of someone until they prove themselves otherwise.

You will feel better about yourself knowing that you have given someone the benefit of the doubt. Do not let negative feelings of guilt, shame, and self-pity build walls of emptiness that you find difficult to bring down.

If you do, you will feel stuck in some kind of lackadaisical approach to life.

To increase your appreciation of these gifts you have to find a way to appreciate the little things in life that most people take so easily for granted.

The simple necessities of living a stress free life. These heartfelt appreciations do not just come to you without some conscious effort to realize and value them. You have to learn to live in the now also learn to let go of the past. Understanding that the future is always changeable.

If you want to right the wrongs that you have done to others you must do two things. First you must be honest and take responsibility for your actions, and you must be specific. Then you can start to mend relationships with others, as well as yourself. Do not resist showing any emotions you feel.

These emotional cleansings free your soul of any feelings of self-resentment that may linger with you.

I remember making amends with my son Jeff. He had been so angry, disappointed, and hurt by my actions.

He was not even speaking to me. After my cancer operation we started to make some contact through the e-mail system in prison. I had mentioned to him that there is a good possibility that some of the things you are angry about I am not aware of, and I won't give you a blanket "I'm sorry" if you will be specific about the things that are bothering you.

All he really wanted was for me to be honest, not make any excuses, and take responsibility for myself. It seems that addicts are always hiding from the truth. People that are in your life can clearly recognize the lies, as plain as the nose on your face.

There is an old saying in AA that "you have to give it away to keep it."

This may seem to be a contradiction but it's true. If you want respect, love, and kindness, then you must give respect, love and kindness.

So to give the gifts of love, compassion, forgiveness, respect, empathy and happiness to others you must first have them yourself. Only then can you give them to others.

You cannot give what you do not have!

No one deserves your best more than your family. They have suffered as much or more than you in your addiction. To be a part *of* your family and not apart *from* your family, you must refuse to live with the constant reminders of the past. If you are reminded by someone about unpleasant past events, stand tall, take responsibility, and admit your wrongs. Reiterate your recovery in life. If you try to justify your past it will make matters worse.

When you are all alone with your thoughts that is the perfect time to meditate on your blessings besides being grateful for all you have. Start to see how you fit in your world. Get comfortable in your own skin. Start to love yourself. Become happy with who you are. Knowing that you are doing the best you can will strengthen your self-image. Being lazy is the worst crime against the human spirit. There is no excuse for laziness. It speaks volumes about a person.

Resist the impulse to live your life by comparison to others. Every one of us has our own dreams, hopes, feelings, and heartbreaks. Everyone's feelings are valid. You never know what happened to that person to shape his or her life. Be kind and understanding in your thoughts of others. Do not be judgmental.

Never throw yourself a pity party otherwise isolating yourself when things do not go your way. Self-pity is one of the most unproductive things to do it serves no purpose.

When you continue striving to succeed even after many set-backs, people will view you as being admirable. That kind of resolve to succeed will build self-esteem, and character. It will give you the spirit of success. Self-pity is a type of self-deception that brings more sadness and frustration into your life. Those negative feelings will only compound your sorrows. I have seen many people in a drunken stupor crying in the lonely corner of a tavern because of self-pity. It's pathetic!

As a matter of fact that is what the Judge that sentenced me said about my behavior. After the Feds arrested me, I was released on bail and put on pretrial probation. It's a program the feds implicate to keep watch on your behavior while you are out on bond. Because I had a drug charge I was expected to report and give urine tests monthly.

While I was out on bond I was getting high as much as I ever was. I knew I was going to go to prison. I had sold drugs to an undercover federal agent. I did not have a leg to stand on in court. So I figured what the hell I may as well get all the partying in that I can.

I would make all kinds of excuses not to report to my case worker.

I once went to the hospital and told them I was having chest pains just to get the wrist band. Usually the hospital puts on the wrist band immediately. My plan was to leave as soon as I got the ID bracelet. I just wanted the wrist band to show the feds why I did not report to my appointment. Much to my dismay they took me immediately to a room and hooked me up to heart monitors.

They kept me there for three days, ran all kinds of tests, and told me I did not have a heart attack and discharged me. Man was I mad.

At a later date, I was out of excuses and my case worker started to threaten me. She said if I missed one more appointment she would revoke me. I went and bought something called synthetic urine. Designed to pass drug tests. I put it in a plastic tube and taped it to my private part.

I went to my appointment with my case worker, knowing that being a female she could not drop me. I was hoping to catch them on a busy day and maybe not have any male available to watch me pee. No such luck. In the bathroom that they make you use has mirrors all around to catch anyone trying to cheat. I started to pee and the man said, "Hey what's that." I said, "Hey man I am trying to go to the bathroom."

He told me to just stop and go wait in the waiting room. I knew he was going to get my agent and she would have me arrested.

I would then be remanded to the federal prison downtown Chicago. As soon as he was out of sight I ran out of the office and into the nearest bathroom and ripped the taped urine tube off my body.

Oh my God what a pain, I muffled a scream and ran quickly to the elevators, I was on the 15th floor, I prayed they would not catch me. I made it out of the building and got on the train home.

As soon as I walked in the house my girlfriend informed me that my lawyer called and said there was a warrant out for my arrest. A friend of mine was also at my house getting high and I told him to grab the dope and let's go to his house.

When we started to leave my house he noticed a car following us. We tried to out run him but the local police were quickly on us. They pulled us over and arrested me. Man how stupid was that.

No thinking of the results, very pathetic.

Think it through. Get in the habit of visualizing the result before you act. It will amaze you how easy thinking in this manner will take hold. It will become second nature. You will see just how wonderful your life is when you can control your lusts and desires. Living in the now does not mean you just go along haphazardly letting things happen as if you have no control. It means you do not squander one minute of your life by giving precious time to useless things. Organize your time carefully so not to waste any of it. Strive to be pro-active in your life to ensure a bright future.

There are many paths to choose in life, and no matter which one you choose, always be true to yourself. Never give into anything that goes against your moral fiber. The way you live your life is up to you. Remember you will have to live by the choices you make.

Do not mistake your wants for needs. Sometimes your desires will lead you down a path you will regret. They often take you places you don't want to go, keep you longer than you want to stay, in addition cost you more than you want to pay.

Just remember the shiniest stones take the most polishing. You will know when you are on the right path because all confusion will leave you, you will feel a contentment and peace that calms your soul.

A life of quality, enjoyment, and wisdom are not birth-rights. They will not just be given to you because of who you are. It will take some thought, effort, and sacrifice to attain the joy life has to offer you. You will have to make a solemn effort to live life to the fullest. You may have to travel down various paths until you find the right one for you.

Subsequently in life, make no excuses, no justifications, take responsibility for your behavior. Adopt the ability to forgive everyone that has wronged you. Respect for yourself will come after you recognize your responsibilities to yourself in life. Above all continually make yourself the most important person in your life.

Chapter Five

The Power of Choice

We are both burdened and blessed by the boundless responsibility of free will and the power of choice. How many times have you wished you could take back a decision, something you said, or relive a minute of your life? I can think of many. I remember one time walking down a street late at night, and a couple I knew passed me in their car, and stopped and asked if I wanted a ride. I knew they were in the drug life, but I needed a ride so I got in the car. We got pulled over by the police about two blocks away. They had drugs and crack pipes on them that they tried to hide under the seats.

When the police got everybody out of the car and separated us, they told the cops that they were just giving me a ride and that all the drugs were mine.

So with my background, I went to jail. I remained in jail for five months unable to post bond. In conclusion, I had to plead guilty to the charges in order to get out of jail, and I was sentenced to rehab plus probation.

We cannot always control our circumstances, however we can choose our responses to whatever arises. Reclaiming the power of choice, we find the courage to live comfortably in the world as we see it. Comprehending that you have the power to change your ways at any moment without regard to external pressures will help you to find self-confidence that will saturate your existence.

When you live by the power of sensible choice you will have clear intentions guiding your life instead of guessing if you are on the right path. Attaining your goals is a process you can break down into a series of small steps. That way you can have many successes along the way.

Each success gives you a rewarding sentiment that will drive you to persevere in doing the next right thing.

Often the finish line seems too far away, and you may want to give up. That is what usually occurs in the effort to change the path you're on. It is essential that you overcome your fear of failure. People rarely fail. They just stop trying.

Every goal in life includes repairs along the way. The road to happiness is always under construction. Enthusiasm sets the pace, but persistence reaches the final goal. Never give up on yourself. The ups and downs in life provide us with consequences and lessons. Sometimes you may have to give up something you want for something you want more. We have many opportunities to learn through cause and effect and to gain life's valuable wisdom.

I can recall a time when I was void of empathy and compassion for people.

I was only out to get something from everyone I met. I could walk in to a tavern and within seconds know exactly who to sit by.

Then as I would start a conversation with whomever was sitting next to me, just a couple of sentences from them, and I would know just how to approach them. What variety of ruse to employ, whether to go with the pity or the aggressive angle, perhaps the happy go lucky person ... it was all a big sham.

You become so many different types of people that you lose yourself in all the deceit. As you get familiar with being deceitful on command, you tend to see the world as though nothing is real. You will become numb to human emotions. It's like you just throw yourself into the streets of the drug world like confetti, and see what crack you fall into. No pun intended.

Empathy and compassion are the recognition of feelings that let us know that we are doing the best we can within the limits of our current beliefs. Conviction when we do something wrong is a signal that we have the precise emotions needed to overcome addiction. Faith is the direct link between our soul and the wisdom that is inside all of us. It lets us know that we are more than just what we have read, heard, or studied.

We need to trust that inner voice that keeps talking to us constantly. Having faith in goodness does not mean trusting everyone to do the right thing. Faith is the knowledge that the spirit of goodness works in all people, even though they may not show it.

There is purpose in pleasure as well as in hardship. Everything that happens to you has a purpose. The dire fact for me is that going to federal prison was the best thing that happened to me at that point in my life.

Actually it saved my life in more ways than one. Had I not went to prison, they would have never caught my cancer until it was too late. I also had a chance to get my mind and body right. I quit smoking, drinking, and drugging the day I walked into prison. Every challenge is an opportunity to grow. I made the choice to not let the time do me. I made the best use of the time to heal myself.

Take heed of those who speak from experience and embrace the knowledge wherever you may find it. I'm sure we all have felt that uncomfortable feeling when we are doing wrong, never the less, we do it anyway.

I wished I had listened to my mother when she would attempt to talk to me about the way I was living my life. I felt so ashamed about my behavior that I would always reply, "I know, I know," and then change the subject. Hearing the truth in regards to my lifestyle did not feel very good.

Our lives are shaped by our experiences in addition to our expectations of ourselves. Our beliefs become the building blocks of our experiences in life. Our beliefs will greatly influence the direction we take in life right down to the friends we choose.

Remember birds of a feather flock together. If you pal around with addicts sooner or later you will become just as your friends. As the saying goes, "If you go to the barber shop enough times, sooner or later you will get a haircut."

Submit to whatever happens in life. Use trials as a learning tool. Remember that surrender does not mean passively tolerating what you don't like nor ignoring injustice, or allowing yourself to be victimized or controlled. Surrender is active, positive, and a creative commitment to make the best use of any situation.

Fighting your problems just gives them energy. Focus on the solutions.

Take the necessary actions to resolve the issue. You will get the feeling that at least you are doing something proactive instead of just leaving it to chance.

There is also a time for doing nothing and letting wisdom prevail. Sometimes no action is the best action. For example, when a couple is arguing it is best to stay neutral. If you choose sides when they make up you will always be the bad guy.

Letting go of all negative attachments within yourself will give you the freedom you need to find your inner peace. Life does not always give you what you expect. Keep your desires in check and know that life is not always about getting what you want, but learning to treasure what you already have.

Promises made to stay clean are made with words, but words do not keep you clean, it is action that brings words to life.

It is easy to talk about courage, commitment, and love. It is easier said than done. Your actions always speak louder than any words you can say. Implementing ideas into actions requires energy, sacrifice, courage, and commitment. Learn when to seize the moments for action. It is so imperative to keep rediscovering the person you are.

As your life evolves, leave behind the useless baggage of anger, fear, envy, and resentments, while understanding that compassion and a love for life can make living more exciting. You do not have to wait to make changes in your life. Nothing monumental has to happen to begin your change. Everyone has the ability to attain the quality of life they desire. The rebirth happens as soon as you change the way you think. You will catch yourself feeling happy to wake up every day, bursting with excitement about what the new day has to offer you. Enjoy!

Chapter Six

Purpose and Meaning

The *purpose* of life is typically a deep spiritual emotion in your heart. It is to be the finest human being you can be. The *meaning* of your life is what brands your individual purpose, gives it a soul, so to speak, or conscience, if you will. You want to pass on to your family your life's experiences, so someone can use that knowledge to make the best decisions they possibly can.

When living in active addiction, your purpose and meaning become the ways and means of getting high. Perspectives become clouded with twisted thoughts of self-justification for your actions. Your life is centered in the subculture of addicts, separate from the rest of the world. You will suddenly know when certain people get paid, receive food stamps, and who got arrested.

I felt so detached from the world that I only became aware of the days of the month as they related to my court dates.

I often had to ask myself what month it was, hell I hardly even knew what year it was.

It will take a lot of courage to change, to liberate yourself from the things that seem so familiar and secure to you. Nonetheless when those things have no more value to you, then it is time to become adventurous, reach out for a new method of thinking. Remember in movement there is life, and in change there is power.

Doing innovative things and thinking in new ways without anxiety of other's opinions is the first step to being your own person, as well as really getting to know yourself.

One fantastic approach to replace all the time you used to spend on addiction is to become a part of something larger than yourself, helping others, whether it be coaching sports, scouting, or Big Brother Big Sister programs. It's a gratifying experience that will bring rewards you never thought possible.

I remember coaching little league baseball on the poor side of town. Most of the kids I coached looked up to their coach as a father figure. That smile on their faces when they get their first hit is a memory that will never fade.

I have kept my friendships with many of the kids I have coached even though they now have children of their own playing baseball. That experience has enriched my life more than words can say. I have so many memories that are both comical as well as touching.

When you are part of youth organizations you will feel young, alive, and useful in the world. You will start to feel a special connection between you and the children you are helping. That bond you share with the children is one of the best feelings anyone can expect out of life.

Your family will begin to look at you in such a way that you will feel a deep sense of pride in yourself. You will become a role model that children will look up to, the kind of person the children can come to no matter what the circumstances, unafraid of telling you the truth no matter how it sounds.

Strive to be the person that gives full attention to someone who is coming to you with his or her problems. Always be humble enough to ask for help when needed besides being able to give it when asked.

Be thoughtful before you speak to children. Be ever so careful to choose your words. Words are similar to bullets. Once you say them, you can never take them back.

The damage will already be done.

There are two instances that have always bothered me. It concerns my oldest son. When he was about six or seven, we stopped at a fireworks store on the way home from a Wisconsin Dells vacation. My son saved up his money to buy some fireworks. He was not sure what exactly he should buy. I was antsy to get back on the road home. So I was rushing him and getting disgusted when he could not make a decision. Then he looked at me with saddened eyes. Then the sales person started rushing him. I wish I could have taken the time with him and helped him in a kind and loving way. That event still bothers me.

Another time was when my son was ten. I was on the phone. At that time we did not have cell phones so I was standing next to a wall phone in the kitchen. And I was in a sour mood from drinking and arguing with my ex-wife. My son came towards me pretending to want to box with me.

I then stuck out my arm and it hit his left shoulder. He fell back and he just looked at me with an expression that said, "Hey what's that all about? I was only trying to have some fun with you." I felt so bad I wanted to cut my arm off right then and there. I remember saying to him, "You better watch who you are messing with," and kept right on talking on the phone. To this day that still haunts me.

When I look back at times like these I feel so ashamed that I did not recognize my role as a father being so vital.

In spite of myself, I am ecstatic to say that today we are the best of friends. We talk everyday, and I am trusted with his most prized possessions, my grand-children. I have keys to his house; I babysit the dog when they are on vacation.

Our life together is great. I thank God everyday for being able to bridge the gap I created between us.

You must begin to listen to your inner-self for direction, learn to follow that voice inside you. It will guide you through the darkest of times with confidence.

Be the type of person that radiates honesty in all you do. Always keep your name in good standing. Lying is most destructive to personal relationships. When you tell a lie it will stay with you forever. It will become the future. When you tell the truth you will never have to worry about what you have said again it will become your past. To lose trust in someone is to lose all hope of a successful relationship.

Make a decision to be happy in your life. You will feel like a new person is evolving. You will seem to walk taller, smile wider, and feel better immediately.

When you choose a new path in life, expect some troubles along the way. Like when you are erecting a building, at first it is extremely difficult to see the finished product.

A similar truth is in your walk during recovery. At first it will be hard to imagine how great your life will become. You must stay the course; keep pushing forward towards the prize of being someone free from addiction. All good things will take some effort to accomplish.

As you change your outlook towards others try hard to not assume anything about others. If you are mistaken it becomes a hard pill to swallow. Do not take the things that others do personal. Most of the time what others do essentially has nothing to do with you; it is all about them.

Avoid confusion in conversations by asking questions, getting all the facts so that you will have a clear understanding of exactly what someone is saying. I know in my life there have been many misunderstandings that have caused extreme problems. I can recall some vicious arguments about what I thought someone said, opposed to what they thought they said.

When it comes to your life never settle for less than you think you deserve. You will be cheating yourself out of the opportunity to be the best you can be.

You will be giving up on yourself. That will lead to inner anger that will destroy your relationships with everyone.

For example if you believe you deserve a raise at work, speak up. Never take that pent-up frustration home with you thus letting it resonate in your family life. Can you imagine as you pull in your driveway after work, your family hearing the car, excitedly saying "Daddy's home." Then you come in with your pent-up frustration and anger. Try to imagine their feelings. Bringing your frustrations home can have a great influence on your family life.

Be attentive of the habits you pick up. Most seem like nothing at first, *the chains of addiction are never felt until they are too strong to break*. You never see the undesirable side until it is too late.

In life we tend to sometimes look so long at the door that has closed for us that we do not see the one that has opened. Many times I have gotten angry over not getting what I wanted or thought I deserved, only to be glad I did not get my wishes. Have you ever been glad about something that did not turn out the way you originally wanted it to?

Or said to yourself how lucky you were that you did not get what you wanted?

One time in particular I was working for a company putting up structural iron in Joliet, Illinois. I was a union ironworker out of the Joliet local. There was not too much work in the area at the time.

So after this job in Joliet, my partner and I were supposed to go to Chicago to erect a building downtown, the Illinois State Building. When the job started we were told that we could not get permits to work there because we did not have union cards out of the Chicago local, although Joliet is only thirty-five miles south.

I had to go out of town to work. I was livid at the time, but as it turned out it saved my life. The ironworkers on that job were in a man-basket that was being lifted up with a large crane.

The basket came apart and all five men in that man-basket died.

That was the most dramatic occurrence, but in reality there have been countless times from wanting cars that turned out to be lemons, relationships that would have turned out disastrous, situations where terrible things occurred. In retrospect, I am so glad some things did not work out like I wished.

Opportunities present themselves all the time. Most of them aren't even noticed until it is too late. I'm sure all of us have at some time in our lives wished we could have a do over. Be aware of the chances that come your way, and when they do be prepared.

All in all remember this: Laugh everyday. Make life fun. Always be a part of your loved ones lives. Have an empathetic ear and an understanding heart for those that come to you in difficult times. Have the wisdom, and strength to give honest advice. Know that each day you have done your absolute best, know that someone has been a little less burdened today because of you.

This is to have succeeded, to give your life purpose and meaning.

Chapter Seven

Life After Addiction

In the wake of a life such as mine floats a lot of

wreckage. A lifestyle filled with drugs and criminal behavior.

Full of lies and half-truths. Time wasted saying and doing

anything to get my next high. I have been homeless. I've lost

everything I owned except for the clothes on my back five

times. I have slept in alleys, old junk cars, crack houses,

shelters, and abandoned buildings. I have been to state

prison twice and federal prison once. I have served several

county jail terms awaiting sentencing, sometimes as long as

eleven months. At one point in my life, I believe somewhere

around 1986, I had in excess of $100,000.00 in the bank, a

house paid for, and two brand new vehicles. By 1994 I did

not have enough money to buy a newspaper, all because of

my crack addiction.

I can remember one time walking to get a $20.00 bag of crack. The bottoms of my feet were cracked because of wearing wet shoes. They really hurt, but the drive to get crack urged me on. I had $18, and I had not eaten in about three days, and as I was walking I passed a KFC.

I contemplated if I could I get a small meal for $3 and still get a $20 bag for $15. As I pondered my dilemma, I thought, why take a chance? So I passed on the chicken. I can also remember drinking out of nearly empty beer bottles and whiskey bottles I would find in the alleys. I used to wake up with my mouth so dry that I would dip my fingers in mud puddles to wet my tongue. You often hear about addicts hitting rock bottom. That only happens when you decide to throw the shovel away.

On one occasion I overdosed myself in the middle of Joliet's housing projects. I was drunk and smoking crack, so to come down from smoking crack I shot up some heroin.

I don't remember taking the needle out of my arm. My friend dropped me off in front of the hospital emergency room. I ended up on life support for three days. When I made it to a regular room the first thing I did was call and try to get some drugs delivered.

Of course no one came. That night in a pouring rain storm I got out of bed and pulled out my IV. Wearing only my pajama pants, t-shirt, and stocking feet, I walked to my house about six blocks away where I believed I left two bags of crack in my garage. I could not find any drugs, so I walked back to the hospital and went to my room and slept soaking wet. The hospital called my family and told them that someone was going to have to sit with me at night. My family responded by telling them not to call anymore. They were done with me. I have never known anybody more addicted to drugs and the life style that it demands more than myself.

My family felt hurt and abandoned. They wondered what happened to the guy who coached baseball, who played games, who made them laugh, who played practical jokes with them. Where did he go? I should have been horse whipped for the way I embarrassed and humiliated my family. The wonderful thing about my family is the love and forgiveness they have toward one of their own. They forgave me once I was recovered.

In the process of making honest and humble amends, your loved ones begin to see the person you once were and they will support you 100%.

The feeling you will get when your family starts to let you back in their lives is so overwhelming. That feeling alone will give you the resolve to do the next right thing. That kind of commitment is very healing to the soul.

I cannot even begin to tell you how peaceful life is for me now. Sometimes it is almost like I am waiting for the next episode of drama to arise. Once you put away the old you and start working on the new person you are becoming you will experience the refreshing sensation of calmness. It seems odd to not be anxious for anything, but living stress free becomes something you will greatly treasure.

It will take some time to get acquainted with this freshly found serenity. There will be days when you will think of your life as boring. You must then think back to those times when you were living in your addiction and everyday was filled with some kind of crisis. Being at peace is not boring. It is a time to reflect on the things in your life that really matter. A time to be thankful for all you now have. A time to take in your surroundings and be enthralled in your life.

That sense of calmness will be a constant reminder of how worthy you really are. Your life will no longer happen at warp speed, always seeming to be on the run and going nowhere. You will feel so much better as your mental and physical health return. If you are blessed enough to still have your health and right mind you can rebuild your life to be even better than before.

In the struggle to remain clean there are two different types of thought, thought controlled either by condemnation or conviction.

Condemnation thinking tells you not to do things because of punishment. Conviction on the other hand will make you feel terrible, because you know what you have done is wrong. Condemnation does not work in keeping clean from drugs. It never has worked and most likely never will. No one ever believes they will get caught. Sometimes jail becomes an acceptable option. Conviction happens when you realize it's wrong to do drugs and to hurt yourself and family. You feel ashamed and guilty.

You will be tempted from time to time. Especially when you go by some of your old haunts, or situations will arise in your life will remind you of getting high. This is a natural thought process since addiction was such a huge part of your life. Usually only the good times come to mind. Be absolutely sure to replay the tape all the way through. I am reasonably sure that none of the so-called good times had a happy ending.

Just because you're now living a clean and sober lifestyle you will still have problems in life, like everyone else. Consider these kinds of problems a joy. To be living life on life's terms. With these problems you can focus on solutions and not worry about going to jail, rehab, or some type of institution.

Your family and friends will now be more receptive to help you besides becoming your support base. You are not in the struggle alone anymore.

Do not look for recognition for doing what you should have already been doing.

Know that you have the power to triumph over those feelings of wanting to relive the old life again. You may think that you can control yourself.

Or that you are somehow smarter now and will never revert to the same behavior that got you so twisted in the first place. Do not fool yourself; nobody can control addiction.

I have tried several times to do drugs under the pretense of controlling it somehow. When that does not work out you will hear those all too familiar words "NEVER AGAIN." If I had a dollar for every time I made that statement. The problem is not getting clean, it's staying clean. There is certainly more than one way to remain clean and sober. There are specific constants that resonate in each method.

Honesty is at the core of all sobriety.

Now that you will have so much extra time on your hands, be adventurous, do new things. Never settle for mediocrity in your life. Take chances, be bold and confident. Begin to have the courage that declares, "I like myself in spite of any outside influences."

Undertaking new things is more exciting than anything the old drug life has to offer. Life will become energized for you. One of the things I chose to do was write this book. Never in a million years did I think I could do this. I joined a writers' group. That was more intimidating to me than going in front of a judge to get sentenced to prison. I recently went to a class reunion. I was the kind of guy that never joined in any school activities. I never did any homework, never took any books home to study. I was the punk that was outside the school smoking and bumming money, trying to act cool.

When I attended the reunion after forty some years, all the people there were a little shocked. And I felt apprehensive. After a few hours they started to warm up to me. Some of the people there reminded me of some of the crazy things I had done in high school. Most of the legendary tales I did not remember.

I knew that I had to start doing things that were new. I must tell you there is a renewed type of excitement in doing activities that you once believed you would never do.

As your new life unfolds, it will feel as though there are not enough hours in the day. As fresh ideas create many new beginnings for you, it will appear as though you are in a constant creative state of mind. The enjoyment you derive by recreating your life will reward you time and time again. You will not have time to worry about your past. You will truly be free from your self-defeating thoughts.

During my renaissance, so to speak, I developed a sincere love for people. It seems to me most people are good-hearted. We are individually so different yet so inherently similar. Life became tremendously more stimulating and entertaining once I developed a warmth for people.

There are also some times when you may encounter someone that you need to make amends with and they may not be receptive to you. They may snub you, or give you the cold shoulder. Do not let it throw you off your square.

They may have been hurt deeply by your actions. It is almost impossible to make a quick amends for that type of emotional wound. It will take time. Allow your actions speak for you. Over time people will notice the change in you.

Addiction and recovery is kind of like playing a country & western song backwards. In addiction you lose everything and in recovery you can get it all back.

I give thanks for my life to God. I have a strong faith in God. I believe that I am an answered prayer. I believe the faith I have helps me to endure the self-doubting and keeps me moving forward on the right path. As you know even if you are on the right track, if you are standing still you will get run over. My prayers are with you all.

Acknowledgments

I want to eternally thank my children: *Anna, Jeff,* and

Joseph. They were the biggest inspiration for this book. Also

my grand-children: *Kierstyn, Sarah, Rileigh*, and *Ashlynn*.

To *Rose Lopez* whom without her this book would

not have been written. She is a wonderful friend and

advisor. I also want thank *Ed Leon* for his constant urging

and inspiration.

To my graphic designer Sue Midlock, and to Denise

Unland for all their help in getting this project published.

Much gratitude to all my friends at **Truth** restaurant,

especially Max, for always being attentive and kind.

My writers group deserves a big thank you, for

listening, editing help, and giving sound advice.

Also much gratitude to Chelsea, my editor she is the best. Her help was such a reassuring comfort to me. Also to Denise and Sue for all their help.

There are so many people that have shaped my life, I want to express appreciation to you all. May God bless every one of you.